Introducing Democratic Socialism to America

By Eteri

DORRANCE PUBLISHING CO
EST. 1920
PITTSBURGH, PENNSYLVANIA 15238

Dorrance Publishing Co
585 Alpha Drive
Suite 103
Pittsburgh, PA 15238
Visit our website at *www.dorrancebookstore.com*

ISBN: 979-8-8872-9249-6
eISBN: 979-8-8872-9749-1

Contents

Introduction

Hello, my name is Eteri. I am from Georgia (country). Georgia is in Europe. I was living in a village called Metekhi, like the Russian president and his mother. Nobody knows where Georgia is, and I will be saying that a lot. I grew up in Georgia and it is a country, people can connect with culture. As a child I liked living in Georgia. Georgian people in America cannot relate history even if there are differences between Georgia and America.

Georgia politics does Russia play in this post-Soviet power struggle, struggles presenting a confident picture of the new Russia. A short distance away, above the Kremlin, the Red Star of the Soviet Union, still in the <u>mausoleum</u> lies the leader of the October revolution of 1917. The Russian President struggles. Putin, the president of the Russian Federation, he rules over a country that even without the former Soviet Republic is still the biggest in the world.... "In front of them or may have died."

It is led by the president of the Russian Federation, who rules over a country that even without the former Soviet Republic is still the largest in the world. Russia as a new government has long since taken over, left across the country, the old symbols are powerful! One, the Soviet Empire encompassed a 6th of the Earth's surface and was home to 218 million people. The collapse of this giant super star in 1991 was an event unprecedented in history and rescinded itself. Fifteen new states have been struggling to find their place in the world order. Some have gravitated toward Western Europe while others look to China, clarified by their relationship to Russia. Instead of the Red Soviet banner today, the Russian flag flies over the Kremlin with the collapse of the Soviet Union, which attracted hopes of liberation and wealth.

Say both sides were loyal abuses but at the Tbilisi rally, only the Russian war crimes are on the agenda, the public humiliation of Georgian soldiers depicted him.

I was heartbroken by Russian soldiers torturing Georgian soldiers in the video. I understand both Russia and Georgia committed crimes against each other, or Georgia did something, but all Georgians have done something wrong just to torture Georgia and psychologically torture. Videos of Russian soldiers abusing Georgian soldiers have made me cry many times. I wish Russians never tormented Georgians and never mocked them and never degraded Georgians again. My heart hurts from emotional distress.

Some Georgians are crying and a world that does not tolerate is inhuman and embarrassing!

Georgia is an independent county but what I heard, Russians razed some territory.

My heart has been broken with cruel inhumanity regarded by the Russians! Mentally I have been going insane. I offer videos for proof of the abuse and psychological torture in Georgia.

This book has inspired me to write from my broken heart, and I am heartbroken from the costs of social rights and torture and human nature. I want to write about the suffering and human nature.

This book has made me cry every day because it is affecting my mental health! Influencing my mood.

Broken heart, like when a loved one passes!

Chapter 1

Political Ideas and Socialism

Walking the aisles of power in Washington, they do not understand that we cannot make healthcare a right for all people, talking about the kinds of things that aren't normally part of the discussion in American politics. We do not shy away from both dialogues of one, they want a stronger social safety net, higher minimum wages paid, rental leave. Alexandria Ocasio Cortez said, "Do not shy away from both conversations of one, they want a bigger social safety net." Her minimum wages, expanded parental leave, healthcare, stronger environmental, now those things don't sound so unusual if you live in a place like Canada or Sweden, the UK or Denmark. Their idea is that we are extreme here in America, a country where universal healthcare isn't even universally approved.

Best believe one would eventually lead to the other America, meanwhile it was a profitable capitalist democracy about as opposite as you could get along the way. Americans became worried that clash of values would eventually lead to nuclear war and the end of the American dream and to the Americans. And so the hunt to root out socialist and communist sympathizers took root at home, and socialist ideals even within the democratic system were effectively ruled out. The main enemy of the United States in the Cold War, of course, was the union of the Soviet socialist men sharing experiences. They could have destroyed the United States' nuclear weapons so not surprisingly, if that's what those were meant for, with turmoil and dictatorship in countries like Venezuela or Cuba, where the government has nationalized industries and where democracy doesn't function, but what America's democratic socialists want is something entirely different. They still speculate in democracy, they don't think the government should be in the business of running businesses and they don't think socialism should be for only anybody (a man's feeling).

American Political Culture

The United States was born free. Its liberation from British rule started where I'm standing, on the village green, and like Louis Harts the United States was born free. Its liberation from British rule began where I am. Thomas Patterson: standing on the village green in Lexington, MA, it was here on a spring morning in 1775 that American colonists first fought the British. Paul Revere had written through the night to warn local militia that the British were marching their way. Militiaman with agriculturists, merchants, and crafts, but the battle came to be known as the "shot heard 'round the world" of civilization who were willing to fight to free themselves of a king from here. The British force marched on Concord seven miles to the west. There they faced off against a larger group of local militia. At this time men on both sides fell as the British marched the 20 miles back to Boston. They were fired upon by Americans positioned in the woods. More than 1000 Americans, one of them 80 years of age, had grabbed their masks and joined the fight. The British were trained to fight in the open field, not against men, protected by rocks and trees. Soon the British were in full retreat when they finally reached Boston, they had lost nearly 100 men, double that of the Americans. On that April day more than two centuries ago, Americans fought for a different form of government, the one where the people would govern themselves. That vision was idealized the year later in the words of the Declaration of Independence: "We hold these truths to be self-evident, that all men are created equal, that they are endowed by their creator."

I grew up in Lexington, been on those greens many times! I am not inspired by Lexington like some people. I have been influenced by inequality and sexual assaults and rape and conflicts of sexism and discrimination, and I do not think most Americans understand sexism, abuse, sexual assault, rape, discrimination, and they need teaching because they all lie and trade off truth! I am not inspired by Lexington, the way someone is or predators who live around me! That green was to be beautiful and most beautiful but conflicts and rebellious people are cruel and nasty.

Lexington being beautiful does not matter because cruel people spoil the peace and glamour!

One place mentions farmers and politics.

Millions of farms that cover the area of 922 billion acres, so as you might have imagined there are also a lot of employees involved in the industry. Without a doubt, high-quality work expects quality accommodations for employees, including a respectful salary. Many farmers today are under a lot of stress because there are many aspects of their livelihood that they can't control and announcements turned on so you don't miss out on any of the new videos we post. First let us talk about how the COVID-19 pandemic affected the farm economy like everything else in the world. The agriculture industry also went downhill because of the COVID-19 pandemic, the new virus is impacting our food system in many ways. Here is what Farm Aid writes about how this matter has been….

Bill Gates on CNBC, walking in at 420,000 acres (about half the area of Rhode Island). America's private grandmaster, largest, there's America, then majority (man feeling).

Wonderful place to live.

Corruption in America

It is believed by one American this:

Present our ideas that everyone this axis represents the likelihood of Congress passing a law that reflects any of these indications from a zero to a 100% would look like this. If 50% of the public supports an idea there's a 50% chance of it becoming law. If 80% of U.S. supports something there's an 80% opportunity. You get the idea. Now most Americans would probably agree that with a few exceptions we should be as close to this idea as possible. Unfortunately the way America actually works doesn't even come close to taking an idea that nobody supports, really nobody, and it has about a 30% chance of becoming federal law. Now taking an incredibly popular idea, the most famous idea this country has ever seen, and there's also about a 30% chance of it becoming law. This means that the number of American voters for or against any idea has no impact on the likelihood that Congress will make it law. Put another way, and I'm just going to quote the Princeton study directly here, the tendencies of the average American appear to have only a minuscule, near 0 statistically, no significant packed up on public policy, so if you've ever felt like your opinion doesn't matter and that the government doesn't really care what you think, well, you're right, but there's a catch. This flatling only accounts for the bottom 90% of income earners in America. Economic elites, business interests, people who can afford lobbyists, they get their own lives. Look at how much closer their line is to the idea, when they want something the government is much more likely to do it and when they don't they look at how much closer their line is to the idea. When they want something the government is much more likely to do it, and when they don't they have the power to completely block it from happening, occurring. No matter how much the rest of the country supports it, they get what they want and guess who ends up paying for it? We pay for it with the most costly healthcare in the world. We pay for it with a tax code.

Poverty has more corruption in America, PBS has broadcasted some: "This very dire emerge program's proven record of accomplishment, it is produced, good housing that is very well run, the crisis, it is property they do not want in their neighborhood and if all the money is going where it should millions of dollars in kick."

It was amazing to me, this is a huge amount of money. If you weren't following the money, how do you know that the low-income housing tax credit is working tonight? Frontline and NPR take a hard look at poverty politics and profit. I never comprehended that a story about low-income housing would lead me here to an upscale resort in Costa Rica. Lo Suenos is a dream world with fancy condominiums and private villas, first-class hotel, golf course, and its own private marina. "I come here (person from documentary informing) because our investigation into the money spent to house more had taken us into a hidden world of secret bank accounts and shell companies, but I'm getting ahead of myself to understand what brought me to Costa Rica. I have to take you back nine months earlier to where our story begins, as our city grows the number of affordable homes is doing the opposite. It shrunk last year. we started spending time in Dallas in neighborhoods like this. We're making rent, has been getting more and more difficult, the struggle is real out here. I mean, you know this is every day for me in a way you down, you know because you've seen it every day. People's rent checks have just been going up and up and up, and I don't see any insight. These are people who have jobs and children, yeah, no, they're saying that no matter how hard they work they still can't find enough here for the roof over their head. This is the vision, right, there are more than 40,000 evictions in Dallas every year. You spoke by phone, an estimated 2½ million across the country, yeah, we get a couple more people here over the past decade, average household income has declined while rents have been rising and that's pushing more and more people."

Horrible. I ended up I didn't want to be here. Credit is like to learn not in the law what happened, a person's emotions, millions of families lost their homes. They involved renters competing in the same rental housing market and at the same time incomes were going down, even for people. Millions of families lost their homes, they became renters contending in the same rental housing market and at the same time incomes were going down. Even if you could keep your job and that led to a rental affordability crisis in this country that's as bad as it's ever been in our history. We come with the dollar, Diane Yentel. One missed day of work away from not being able to pay the rent. They're really at risk of losing their homes altogether and becoming homeless.

"people without homes."

"Only one in every four households that are eligible for and in need of housing assistance."

Dallas from PBS, welder, clerical work stuff like that, but even when working she says it's been hard to find a place she can afford. "What did you think when you got about?" "I thought this is freaking awesome, yeah, I felt like it was a chance for me to game."

PBS: "Elsewhere we kept hearing about the largest of the program's Section 8 voucher/"

Los Angeles Homeless on People and Their Stories!
Downtown Los Angeles, there is trash everywhere plus homeless people. Poverty and malnutrition and stunting and poor healthcare. There are lots of concepts of poverty in Downtown Los Angeles! It is not okay, people, to be hungry. It breaks my heart to see people hungry one way or the other. I am not looking at evil when I feel pain, I am not doing evil when I feel pain; I do not commit evil, but pain does not act evil. So, I feel lots of pain for these Downtown Los Angeles homeless people, being homeless, no food, hungry, and poor, and it is just extremely evil, violated, and challenging. These people grieve so much with mental issues and living and are the poorest in America. There are lots of other homeless in America, but this is not acceptable! It is so immoral to live this poor! My heart is in pain and I am crying every day, feeling so much sorrow!!

Watching many videos, I have been in California, when I was only teenager, and San Francisco, not Los Angeles; however, some man was telling me, Francsico, "I want to take you to Downtown Los Angeles!!" Ha-ha, I had no idea what he was talking about. I was like teenager and different teenager, did not speak as good English, I was from Georgia, so I had no clue about English and anything else in America and their evil or English, period!! I hope he was not talking about showing me conceivable poverty and drug issues and mental issues!! This makes me cry and it is distressing!! I do not know what he was talking about. Was he on drugs?

I have seen some homeless in Amecia and I never been in Los Angeles, but it would make me cry! I feel like there are mostly Africans that are homeless in Los Angeles!! I do not know what is up!

African Segregated Issues and Abuse or Racial Issues

One documentary informs this story about black people.

There are only a few meters apart but the people on each side live very many lives. There are only different lives. There are only a few but the people there are only a few meters apart, but the people on each side live very distinct lives. Strand has backyards and driveways, strand driveways from it is much more dense and the people here have fewer basic services and less piped water, internet access, and non-Zamo is majority black while the.area across a line is preponderance, white and non-Zamo is white and non-Zamo is plurality black while the area across a line is majority white. If the dude who was telling his story, saying, "We use dots on a map to depict rates, if we use dots on a map, if we zoom out to the whole city we can see it's actually everywhere, if this is the case across (man speaks his experiences) South Africa there's the color of your skin here, it often differentiates," how the jobs and opportunities are primarily concentrated who came to town. It also determines your quality of life. This word shows how the jobs and chances are primarily concentrated, who came to town. It also determines your quality of life. This word shows how the jobs and opportunities are primarily centralized, who came to town. It also determines your quality of life, and this is where most of the city's black people live, in informal settlements called townships on the cities' peripheries, transported for up to three hours a day in there. Can't take care of the responsibilities in the community with the rest, even better because they are always working and they are always traveling for decades.

South Africa was under apartheid, a system that wrote segregation into people. They have to move by public transport for up to three hours a day because they are always working and they are always traveling for decades in segregation into a white minority control.

There is degradation in South Africa and there are racial issues in America too.

African racial issues, "We are streaming this live on the websites of the forum." The man in the documentary witnesses the progress of black people. "Also participate in a live chat that is now going on before letting us take a yolk. All video quality but you about young colored, you can also partake in a live chat that is now." The chat meaning that on his videos people can join the practice.

Colored foundation, it was shot 2000.

One African person says, "I had an extremely high rate like transfer like conforming folk black woman like."

Second African person says, "Men, we are on things that make us look better, close, click, release offices."

Third African person from the documentary says, "There isn't something else that's pushing you toward the edge, you got everybody against."

Africans are big faces of the poorest people and cause of poverty around the world and in America! It is not fair, there should be fairness in the world! Africans should have equality and independence like whites! There should not be a doubt in that! It is such a miserable feeling and miserable life to see humans unhappy and suffering from hunger and having issues with their health! 1. Inequality; 2. Conflict; 3. Hunger, malnutrition, and stunting; 4. Poor healthcare systems.

Poor people suffer and live in extreme poverty, it is so sad and contempt. Poverty affects the socializing and people, its health and other conditions ... effects of the poverty are sad, and it is painful. It gives people a feeling of sickness and no smile. I hate that. People cry and people cry because of sadness and they cry out of pain.

Poverty is a complex problem. There are many aspects to it, and it has many causes. The most widely used poverty definition focuses on economic poverty.

White People's Feelings and Thinking, "Prevalence within Africa"
"On any given day in 2016, an estimated 9.2 million men (about half the population of New York), women, and children were living in modern slavery in Africa. The region has the highest rate of prevalence, with 7.6 people living in modern slavery for every 1,000 people in the region."

That is incredibly sad to see that Africa would have salves! That is heart-wrenching! However, Africa is not America! It is believed in America, by people and their perspective, that Africa is different and is abusing its own black people! Their South African system is disliked! There are no inequalities in black lives, some whites think but there is race and ethnicity barriers to blacks. There is white supremacy in America, some blacks think. European cultural and politics are disliked by Americans, but neighborhood significances, white racial attitudes and there are some black people's social and economic and political lives that are influencing their lives. Blacks are affected by white Americans.

In America there is no slavery, some white Americans say, and blacks are making up their attitudes against them and blame! Most whites think blacks are racist and not them! I feel like most white people are abusive and rude! I do not believe them and their aptitudes of manipulative behaviors! As a white person myself, I find whites manipulative so if they were to have something to say their theories are manipulative and narcissistic! I do not believe them at all!

There are rude and generalities of effects on attitudes and there are narcissist whites! There are rude white people in America!

They lie and they have trouble lying and manipulating things and deluding to be nice!!
Okay, even though America has laws, which slavery was not banned nationwide in the United States until the Thirteenth Amendment was ratified on December 6, 1865. The Act Prohibiting Importation of Slaves on 1 January 1808 made it a felony to import slaves from abroad.
Which many Africans are happy, I am sure of that; still, there have still been lots of problems with years and long times with discrimination against blacks! So, I know white people are twofaced, fake, hypocritical and even liars, so they have not been nice to black people! White people are two-faced! Being two-faced and crazy! (Not all of them but about all strangers and acquaintances!! Enough that is a problem!)

Be Such a Beautiful Soul That People Crave Your Vibes

"For four hours that type of trauma really seeks it to, the soil of opinion, the thing about Ferguson we must remember is people were not just disputing the death of an unarmed black, people were protesting rep revenue rating policing and some."

Kayla read: "For justice requirement in the city I was a pharmacy technician that went out because she did not believe this happened by this table for justice requirement in the city that went out because she did not believe what transpired by this table for justice regulation. I need an organization that is constructing offensive power. Ferguson is to meet lots of the racialized history."

Reporter: In a quick refresher in episode one of this series, he explained how the bail system works. You pay money to the court to get out of jail while you wait for your trial but if you cannot afford it you stay in jail and pay money (Kayla read) and Kayla says, "We are likely to be pulled over, we are taking it, we are more likely to be arrested, we are more likely to be convicted, we are more likely to be sentenced to death, that's across you know. I have faith."

Reporter in Saint Louis: "Black residents are twice as likely to be arrested as white residents." I have faith in Saint Louis.

Chapter 2

Ukraine Exposing Racial Disparities, Ukraine Conflicts: Students and People Facing Discrimination and American Crises around the World

Ukraine War Is Exposing Racial Disparities

I watched the Daily Show and this was what it mentioned (perspectives and pacts) on the video: "What I'm still showing is some amazing sympathy and little answers and all the chaos created, humanity still prevails. This video is going viral this morning, appearing to show Ukrainians helping to capture the Russian soldier, giving and allowing him to call his mother to tell her that she's okay, she's right there in the hat, the soldier fighting back, fighting back tears and only telling his mom."

My perfectives, I do agree with the Daily Show, Trevor Noah, this was crazy about this. Videos about Ukrainians being nice toward Russians! I comprehend they want to be and have compassion and be respectful and politeness, but this was only a spit in the face, Russians killing so many people and they have killed many people in Ukraine and the reason Trevor Noah was talking about this is also black exposing racial issues and yet, Ukraine wants to be nice toward Russians? I understand his feeling about this circumstance. I have watched many attacks by Russians on Ukraine. Ukraine goes to being nice to Russians, okay, not every Ukraine was nice to Russians, but the idea is that if you have war you have to shoot your enemies. Not that I do not enjoy good compassion, but I do not see kindness in America! But Russians get kindness and compassion by some women in Ukraine? Haha! I do not see Americans' honor and empathy, but Ukraine wants to be nice to Russians?

It is just scary to be nice to Russians when they are killing people and raping people! It is so painful and sad and Ukraine, your lesson needs to be shoot your enemy, ha-ha!

So black people face so much by this Russian war! Racist cases in Ukraine: gravitas: commissioner for refugees is now substantiating to us cases of discrimination in admitting refugees, one Congo native saying screaming and being discriminated against while trying to board a train out of Ukraine, take a commissioner for refugees are now confirming to us cases of discrimination in admitting refugees for refugees, one Congo fight for Ukraine, "We are going to fight for Ukraine because we are blind because row from double."

News reporter: "Trying to leave, attempting to leave, trying to leave just south of trying to get off, trying to get off just south of that bar there are, just send it, send it, send it only motivates that we're headed west that saw that there were white men who were allowed to get on but that the species of color were barred from getting onto that train and it was a moment of disbelief. You know now there have been several reports of discrimination that have unraveled that get stuck in this mass exodus. Do you expect to be treated a certain way so on a certain level he was not shocked by what happened but necessarily it was sad."

Mark, same person, regauges: "Why black, that's why, black, that's why, black, that's why, come on, we are black people, you know why, people, you already know we already know we stop."

Reporter Markus, news perspective and repeated voices: "Person that they are seeing two to be a unique experience for them and that at one point some of them were just pushed, instructed and shot and beaten is what he said so but then he said that if we will appear to be from Africa, man or woman, that they are seeing two to be a various experience for them and that at one point some of them were just pushed, urged and shot and beaten is what he said so but in particular he said that if we will appear to be from Africa, man or woman, that they're seeing two to be a different experience for them and that at one point some of them were just pushed, instructed and shot and beaten is what he said so but in subject to clear discrimination and even tonight, Kira, we have heard reports of events where people who appear to be from Africa have been harassed by members left that you were subject to clear racism and even tonight, Kira, we have heard reports of incidents where people who appear to be from Africa have been victimized by members' countries even tonight."

It is gross and unfair how black people are being treated with the afflicted and lying in Ukraine with this Russian war! It is so sad seeing these black people facing racial bigotry and it affecting their lives and they are being shot and beaten! I have seen many Ukraine conflicts: related to African children undergoing abuse, racism, hunger and being cold and not having home and safety and many other situations families are encountering, no privacy, serenity, and safety! This is incorrect, blacks to have the safety and freedom and privacy and respect by anyone and white people are not special, not that where they kill people and put their lives in harm!! The Ukraine war has been hard to not sob and cry over abuse and rape and shooting and blacks being affected by violence and shooting, and this war has impacted blacks' lives badly in Ukraine: The Russian war has caused conflicts: Africans' racism and being killed and who knows how many killed? Children with no homes and affected by the trauma and conditions that are not good! War circumstances always suck but war and random people's violence against blacks and their pig police shooting black people and they are not able to get out of Ukraine with humanitarian support and police and all other support they should get!! It is not okay, white or black child, to not get support by police and people who are supposed to be leaders! It is not okay, white or black child, to be raped and sexually raped and be hungry and cold and freeze! This is so wrong and so beyond okay! It makes me so upset to hear and see that in Ukraine there is some (at least during the war of Russian invasion) racism happening and killing innocent black people and children and students. I do not care who they are and how old, it is not okay to kill innocent black people just like it is not okay killing innocent whites!!

My heart breaks to see abuse and rapes and physical consequences of post-traumatic and anxiety and effects on Africans! All of them, who have been affected by this Russian invasion war! I feel sad about Africans' death, injury, sexual violence, malfunction, illness, and many other issues by the war and the issues in Ukraine about racism (outside America), not only just any old racism but killing, deaths!! This is heartbreaking and it is shameful! I understand not everyone is racist, I am not dumb! But it is wrong to be racist and whites are not best and better! Nowhere should whites ever proficiency to cause death and injury!

I wish the kindness toward at least the black people who did survive in

Ukraine, it is few problems that cannot be fixed, it is damaging mentally once who did get killed. Trauma is damaging my life too. It is detrimental and damaging to kill someone and abuse someone! Racism is detrimental and prejudicial too!!

Children should not be injured and killed by racist reasons and war or anything! Little children are so innocent!

A video I watched for blacker people's backgrounds toward other people and Georgia in the country too!

"Today we're going to be reacting to you actually been being black in Germany according to the video, so I'll be relating it through my own place because I'm a student, currently Georgia listing."

"Experience is wrong, this is what I went through, and I just want to let you guys know how it was for me. Let us get strictly to the feeling, as you can tell from the title this video is going to be about being black in Germany and coming from my experience what I went through living here and I think. Experience is wrong. This is what I went through and I'm unhurried. Germany is on the staring so my God, this is actually true like this text, so I'm lagging Germany is on would sample so the first thing that they start at and the way they start, she's like this test so as "they look straight into your eye like there's nothing you can do about it or you know why you solve that somewhere, you don't want them to know you are staying at them but these people know they stacked like yes, I'm looking. They look straight into your eye like there's nothing you can do about it."

Also, so I do not know if it is a cultural thing or something because I am very shocked at first as looking like they have never seen a black person before.

I'm very shocked at immediately but I found in Germany at the southern park where I lived, they are just still so hard that if you stand back at them, they don't look away like they'll just staring at right. But sometimes it is a little bit like damn, do I have like ketchup on my face, but obviously that is not it because it is because I am black. I am black, with that I want to bring up to you guys this kind of ignorant comment you see. They look away when you step back at them, they are just looking weak so yes, nothing and it is just sometimes everything, it's all coming down to race, that's everything we always attach it to, being the black race that's everything, we always attach it to being black, yes, it is like I felt so bad just got other.

But they have these one-in-a-million people who you will possibly encounter but again this is not saying that Germany is a racist country or anything like that, but I'm saying but they have these one-in-a-million people who you will possibly encounter.

"But in general, so please thank Tbilisi, Georgia, the welcoming city for a black person."

I am happy to hear that Georgia is not racist and at least these black women did not have a racist experience. They just feel like being black speaks the racist! I do feel like in Georgia there are fewer dishonest people and lying and racists overall, but it turns on a person's ordeal! Overall, there are fewer occurrences like UN-FAIR, dishonest, lying, untruthful, backbiting, bent, bluffing, disingenuous, insincere, artful, crooked, cunning, foul, corrupt, but again, I have not lived in Georgia, and I was a child leaving from the country so I cannot say if a black person would have a terrible experience in Georgia and have a terrible experience! But I do know Georgia and I know Georgia is my country and I know it with my brain and language. I forget the language or there is other language in Georgia I have not learned, but I have lived in Georgia eleven years! I still know a little Georgian, which is crazy! I have the reality of Georgia and language and Georgia's way but at the same time I have not been there a long time! But I will always be Georgia, so at least two people are having a pleasant experience in Georgia while they are black, that is good! I am happy to learn that Georgia is fair toward black people, and I am not sure Georgia has bad people, but I do know lots of people are fair and cool!

I am happy to hear Georgia is being fair with blacks! I did live in Georgia and was beaten and treated unfairly a lot! Haha, but not all Georgians' fault, it was really my biological mother's issues and her boyfriend, not the entire community and society! Georgia has some bad people, but those people are not seen from America!

I watched random videos about someone's statements of Georgia, and it does affect me like how I go through in American racist issues myself, and abuse, and injustice and the same ways black people do and exploitive behaviors of Americans and all people I know in America! They are racist and exploitive and taking advantage of me always and taking advantage and attacking me one way or another, my booty or sexual harassments. I have been raped many times and in America rape is common and psychological abuse and coercion and genocide! Overall, in America there are rude people and people who are racist and who have problems mentally and are trash! It has been hard to live this country with rapes, genocide, and being abused emotionally and there are lots of problems with everyone in this country! But in Georgia someone goes there, and they have the experience of Georgians treating me well, kindness, generosity, and respect! This is upsetting because I have lived in Georgia, damage, and Americans (and bad Americans do not deserve kindness, generosity, and respect). I understand that not everyone is bad. I understand I feel angry, but still, I feel one way and kindness should not be okay with trashy Americans and people who attack me and disrespect me! I want to kill myself every day because of the genocide and hate and abuse and malpractice and misconduct and negligence and abandonments and sexual abuse and rapes and so many other issues! But Georgians are nice to random people who are in America, two-faced and wrong and mentally crazy and mentally ill and are crazy and offensive and criminals! It just affects me mentally, my mood!! Georgians should not be nice to scumbags and criminals and mentally ill people!

So, I am envious of Georgians being so nice to strangers but hear what these people's feelings are about Georgia:

"One of my favorites in the world now, he has tasty food, beautiful views, and it has many opportunities for it, but it is manageable, it is effortless, it still feels relaxed! Backstreets and hipster areas with paintings and graphics all over, the woman stayed in one of these areas most full of urine, all of Europe's beauty of Georgia is remarkable that in my mind anywhere quite like it where you Fred, then Georgia, chakapuli, which in many ways are favorites, this both boats, the red filled with cheese and an egg yolk and butter, and I mean it is not good for the yard to the arteries, just so our favorites, which is many."

People who visited Georgia have spoken of those things, but I feel jealous because when I lived in Georgia I never got to do those things and I feel sad. Income through living in Georgia and I are chakapuli but not all the time! Years would happen and we would struggle and starve and were hungry. It was sad in Georgia going through abuse and neglect and lacking food. More than lacking, we would starve and have serious conditions! I just do not know how I have survived. But I did not get to see beautiful mountains I did, but I did not do ziplining mountains. I am heartbroken about this.

Traditional Georgian Food

Khinkali (Georgian Dumplings): Beautifully twisted knobs of dough, khinkali are typically stuffed with meat and spices, then served boiled or steamed.

Badrijani Nigvzit

Lobio (Bean Soup)

Qababi (Kebabs)

Dolmas

Chakapuli

Mtsvadi (Shashlik, meat skewers)

Satsivi

I find it wrong that I experience genocide and bodily harm and other harm in America and by American people, and even if I do not know everyone in America, I still do not want to skip anything else. I have not had good experiences in America with racism and hate and genocide and people trying to attack me physically and mentally and doing bodily harm!! But it is unfair Americans can visit Georgia, anyone, and blacks do not receive the same genocide and receive in America. This feels really upsetting! However, what can Georgians do? Act like Americans and act without morals and unethical? Not every American but this is mostly about violations and human injuries related to American people and people who disobey and people who have been through genocide, been trying to do bodily harm and mental harm and affect my living commotion to destroy me!! So even if there were great people in America, well, I do not know you!! I never thought about it. This is about America, who caused me serious bodily and mental harm based on their genocide! So, I am angry and frustrated. I want to kill myself every day. I cannot deal with damages! It is just unfair!

I want to kill myself every day! I go mentally insane with trauma!! I cry every day and I scream pain out daily!! Americans have destroyed me!! I am jealous of Americans!! They get what they want and like and they are selfish and greedy (ones I know are)!

I find it unreasonable that in America I experience genocide, antiracism, and bodily harm and harm people do against me and have but in Georgia, they are welcoming, kind, compassionate, and friendly!

On BBC Broadcasts, Africans' Opinions about Discrimination and Racism

Africans are caught up in the horror of the war in Ukraine. Students are not fighters. This is not our war, it's not our fight, you want to go, you want to go? As they flee many will be treated as second-class citizens, yeah, not allowing anyone to arrive inside Ukrainians, that's all that if you are black you should walk. It was hard, it was uncalled for, it was deeply inhuman. This is not our move, it's not our fight. Once I speak to the parents and the predicament of war is when every single person he's trying to escape and to struggle.

Americans have lots of pain associated to Ukraine being unfair (that is what Africans). That Ukrainians are unfair and racist too and even other countries, but Ukraine too. They do not feel like they are Ukraine. Africans do not feel the Russian war is their war! Fleeing is their issues and safety, and anger is not showing yet about deaths because fleeing is their priority while the building is on fire. Africans are sad and suffering by the Ukraine war plus Ukraine being racists. Wishing not everyone but it is hard to separate good and bad during the war (invasion and killing).

This racism against Africans in Ukraine is sad! It breaks my heart! I have seen many black people cry and children! It is most derogatory and humiliating!

Chapter 3

Democratic Socialism, Black People, Georgia, World

A chilling word in the United States, it helped fuel the red scare when Congress carried out massive witch-hunts to weed out suspected American communists and traitors after each World War. Our job as Americans and as Republicans is the dysplastic printers from every place where they have been sent to do their treacherous work until previously, though socialism had been referred to the sidelines of American politics and it has taken more of a positive when I talk about democratic socialism.

Bernie Sanders said, "I am talking about Medicare when I talk about Democrats or not."
Subsidizing college for all students in America, students' opinions on what they say about Sanders "really resonate with my workers' rights."

"Climate change, he's planting the seed, closing the wage gap."

"He cares about black students on this campus movement that's going to exist for many years." To understand democratic socialism in America, it is best to start with the basics: capitalism, awesome; and communism, awesome; and communism exists along an economy.
There are economic issues in America I have observed, expenditures and deficits:

Social Security
Family income
The savings rate

Biden's plan for Social Security: The plan would reduce the conventionally measured long range in balance by 1.5% of taxable payroll, leaving an imbalance of 2.0% to the line to decrease.

For example, when both spouses previously received equal benefits the surviving household's benefit is cut by 50% because many household expenses are not divisible. This causes steep reductions in survivors' living standards, the plan for career workers' efforts that based on efforts historical earnings' efforts lower earnings, transportation and personal assistant services increase at old ages.

Thus, suffer declines in living, those who live through incredibly old age often live longer than they expected and saved for and thus suffer deteriorations.

I have been dealing with hunger, food insecurity for long time, and while there is obesity and chronic disease and diabetes I am not saying people who have chronic diseases are bad people, but I am speaking about my experience lacking food and risks of that! I collect SSI today, as of July 27, 2022, and that is not enough for money for food! It is risk in hunger, not obesity! But I am not saying people cannot gain with. I am not happy with my weight but that is due to aging, other physical impacts and trauma and stress, anxiety, and depression. I have sadness and grief. I am affected by mood disorders. Sadness, I also have anger, if anybody takes away situations and events.

Family income, poverty and uncertain and irregular employments, erratic housing, public benefits, shifting households' compositions, healthy issues, wellbeing of people, lacking education and lacking access of jobs ... and lacking justice and there is social injustice (alimony, child support and workers' compensation, education, financial, public assistance and welfare, retirements). These are all not enough support and sources are not enough money for support, and getting by and issues, biggest issues, food insecurity, inadequate childcare, lacking access of healthcare, unsafe neighborhoods, and adversely impacting and unsafe neighborhoods exist (Boston anywhere Cambridge, Lexington, Waltham, Burlington, and all cities). Everyone seems to think that dangerous neighborhoods are always something that nobody really related to and its unknown region. It is known that there are dangerous people in Boston and Cambridge, Waltham, Lexington, and every city! So, it is made up of pathological lying and lies that these cities are safe! Yes, if you stay inside your home! But there are bad and dangerous and criminal people and people who are looking and seeking rape often! Women are most usage in these cities! It makes up lies, these cities where nothing bad happens and no actives! That is lies and women are affected in most activities!

This is a disorder that afflicts a percent of the world's population that we as a society know little about it. Stereotypes tell us that depressed people are weak unless they happen to be a tortured artist. It can be difficult to understand depression because it's invisible, it's a disorder defined by thoughts, behaviors and feelings rather than obvious symptoms like vomiting, rashes or fever. Those who have undergone depression are all too familiar with comments from misguided friends such as "Snap out of it" or "Just get up and do something." Even those with depression might have a hard time understanding what they are experiencing and they often blame themselves for not being able to snap out of it, to understand what depression really is. We need to talk about symptoms or to understand what depression really is. We need to talk about symptoms. First of all, sadness has symptoms related to how someone feels. These symptoms include nearly constant feelings of sadness and anger!

I do not have a family with depression because I do not have a family, and my real family never had depression, so I do think it is my family did not pass to me depression! I was adopted and I did not come to America with depression and ID name in America with any of the issues:

Hearing Loss

Hepatitis A

Hepatitis B

Hib Disease

Influenza (Flu)

Intellectual Disability

Jaundice (Kernicterus)

Kernicterus (Jaundice)

I came to America without taking drugs and had standard send that was achieved in Georgia as a human! I was the age, ethnicity, culture, ability, and gender—all these standards came from Georgia! When I was eleven, I had more standards than American people! That's how in Georgia I was raised with standards and how I would say.

In America standards are different, especially with low, degraded people, and who do not act right and are trash! Some people have more standards than others in America!

My depression began in America and the risk of depression came from suffering in America! American issues and events in America! I have experienced backstabbing, deceit, disinformation, duplicity, falsehood, fraud, hypocrisy, and lying about my mental issues in America, including acting like my depression is FAKE!!!!

While they misuse me in America and deceive me and abuse me, they also lie and make up things and pretend mental illness is in my head, "even though fake and not real."

Africans also feel like whites are racist, but I am white. Whites are trash and not everyone. I am never including good people in racism and doing wrong. There is white trash. In America there is lots of it and I would like to say that it is not okay, these people cause harm, and they are affecting Americans! They have affected me and destroyed me! These people are not just affecting blacks! These trashes have the ability to affect anyone and anybody!

These trashy people are very jealous and have bad tempers and are controlling and use people! They are angry and they are dishonest, and they are abusing drugs or people or different while women are FALSE and bad parents and jealous men are more abusive and users and violent and rude and more jealous and more manipulated and more controlling and more narcissistic, more inconsistent and critical.

It is not just blacks' experience that sucks with white people. Crazy white people are mentally unstable and are liars and explosive and have bad tempers! I am not sure how blacks would like all information about white people.

I have low self-esteem by being lonely, and molestation, rape and abuse, you name it! Being black might be the worst! (I am sure it is bad but just saying it is the worst affecting you or your family? Is it worse than strangers abusing you or your family?) Struggles with domestic violence, do they think that's better than being black in America? I am sure being black is disastrous in any characteristic of abuse, but domestic violence and some other stuff is bad too.

Domestic abuse and mental abuse and that is bad too and stress and all other stuff. I have been raped by black men, hmm, America has not given me justice for that! It is humiliating! It is emotionally damaging, and I would like to be shot dead! I don't see that being related to blacks and I am not saying all black is bad and it's obviously unrelated, the hate I go through to blacks. But it does suck to go through rapes and black men raping me, that is damaging and that is racist and that is to destroy me! I have gone crazy by my experiences! I cannot keep up with the harmful and hurtful issues in America! I have been living my life with damage and I am suffering every day in America! Blacks do not care, and I am not saying everyone is bad, but it is also obvious my issues that I am suffering are not black people's issues and their trauma....

It is hard emotionally to deal with trauma, and I am a mother only to one child, and black people have more than one child and the reason I find it unfair is because I only have one. They will argue that is enough, when, how? If I was sexually active since I was child, I should have a lot more. It is no one's business how many children I have but I am getting so frustrated and upset about my feelings when they do not care about what I think! Nobody does, they keep using manipulations, affecting me daily!

That concludes psychotherapy and medication, either can work on their own but to be the most productive in summary, gloom is a disorder that is widespread but poorly understood. The symptoms can negatively affect a person's thoughts, feelings and behavior to a debilitating degree; however, there are treatments.

I do not see how it is poorly understood when I have understood everything?! You get depressed with abuse and abusers abusing you and by the dumbest people, so when you get abused you will get depressed. Bad abuse should affect the person and stupid persons abusing you will change your mood! So, there are many stupid people who harm me and that is depression affecting me. It affects the brain in diverse ways, self-esteem and depression and anger and anxiety and PTSD, CPTS, trauma?! I have lots of trauma by stupid people abusing me! So, I think we poorly understand depression!

I don't have issues understanding depression.

So, I have trauma in my head. I have no proof of that either and that might be PTSD and depression, even though I am still a happy person and I still try to do my best to be happy and have happiness. I have strength, hope.

I am the person who will have strength to do something good in life and I am the happiness in life, and I enjoy life and I am joy. I love people being happy! I am positive person, I like positive people! I do not like drama! I do not like issues, and I do not like sadness! I work hard being positive and super positive!! I do not like unhappiness!! I am all about joy, excitement, and love. I love feeling happy. I am always happy because I do not expect anything from someone. I am even more happier making others happy and being there for them and taking care of them. I love taking care of people. It gives some happiness instead of nothingness. Being there for people gives me worth.

Yes, I struggle but nobody sees my struggles! I keep myself stable and do right things and I do not do wrong things. I do not rape people and lie to people, and I do not use people! For me that is good stability to not use people! I am also not the most wanted criminal, and I did not rape anyone like a lot of the dumbest people do! I do not do illegal drugs either. I am sure not all people who do drugs are weird, but I just want to say something about myself not caring about criminals and the dumbest people.

Elaborating on the dumbest people in America, well, there are a lot of them and they are murdering people or raping people, and some are suicidal because of bodily harm and abuse and other malpractices and other moments! Gynecologist malpractice, well, I have experienced that. I am afraid to go to the doctor and they have harmed me with that in many ways! They have damaged me and are risking my life from suicide to going to the doctor. What if I die with a disease and not a gynecologist appointment? They do not care, and they are not thoughtful! Domestic violence and abuse of children and all other abuse! These is lots of abuse. I have deeply been disturbed by American life!

I am sure even Britney Spears has been going through rough times in America! She has been my favorite since the age of eleven! I was shocked to see someone beautiful like Britney Spears when I was younger, but by the time I was teenager I did not like Britney because of anger and abuse caused by trauma and brain damage on my head! Finally, I love Britney Spears again. I am sure she has more important stuff than caring about strangers, but I just like her music and I support her strength and abilities of being real person and how just kind she is in my eyes. I wish her the best and only doing well. She is in my eyes the greatest!

You can imagine the issues I have received being abused in America! It is hard dealing with abuse I have gotten in America ... I want revenge and I want to repay. I just want my justice!!

I was watching videos of documentaries and some homeless people have spoken their feeling about their families' struggles and the pandemic and federal eviction and other stuff… their voices about people, needs and people's perspectives.

This is what a homeless woman spoke about the homes during the COVID pandemic and her family and daughter and family: "We're unprecedented over the course of the year in states across the country and inside. Look at the housing crisis during the pandemic from those affected the most. There's a patchwork of eviction policies that state much of the attendance experience was completely conditional upon the zip code that they lived, millions of Americans who've gotten behind on their rent incomes during the pandemic. These are people that have jobs that have felt secure, not from frontline people for free. I need to see that our government cares equally about landlords, they do with tenants is taking for.

"I came home with a 20 yesterday. I came home with a 24-hour notice to vacate on my door. Yesterday I came home with a 24-hour notice to vacate on my door. I have a 5-year-old, so you know, just trying to appreciate trying to understand the list."

This woman's piece about homelessness and struggles triggers me, my strugglers typo in America. I struggle from psychological trauma, and to protect them the federal government ordered billions in rent relief and a temporary ban on evictions first through the CARES Act, which made her through a moratorium issued. By the precedented move the Trump Administration announced a temporary national moratorium on evictions for tens of millions of renters who've lost work over the course of a year. We went to states across the country to see how the protections were being carried out. Time is running out to keep families from being kicked out of their homes.... I was homeless too and my son and I were homeless too. This homeless woman's expenditure really triggered PTSD and anger: feeling anger!! I have felt lonely and vulnerable since age eleven in America and I have felt lonely and venerated from ages 11, 12, 13, 14, 15, 16, and permanently. (My anger was not like a police shooting because I did not shoot! I was angry and I am. But I have not shot anyone, and I have not committed wrong. But I am still angry.)

I have trauma triggers about my son and him, affected emotions and bodily sanitations and affected his little body to the conditions and trauma. I have an anger feeling that my son should have never been homeless! My heart is broken with this trigger! Trauma is really a trigger! My trigger anger memories feeling abandoned, frustrated and tension. Yet, I still 24/7 manage myself being happy and

I have strength to be happy. I want revenge and I want justice, but I do have strength and that strength has kept me alive and my heart can and will uphold you.

I have a son. I want him to live his life happy and I want him to be strong and live a great life! I pray to God that he lives happy and has strength! I will do anything for my son Jason, and I will give him strength and I will be there for him! I will help my son. My son is joy, and my son is better than trash. He is a wonderful person and his heart is great, and his heart is for love and joy!

Homeless in America: This is a big problem in America and involving Americans driving by these homeless people and none of them (sure, here and there give them something, a gift of a jacket, not enough. They need to wear like several layers of sheep fur to get by, but they do not give them enough blankets to sleep outside!), and while Americans drive and pass by all these homeless people, none of them help! Help is when someone is able to help someone through poverty, through positivity and income and being poor. There are too far issues and problems to have overtly and homeless in America! There should not be homelessness in America! These people have family, and they are living in America as citizens! One person cannot be more important than another person! So, poverty is impacting these people and while there are rich people, and I call you rich if you have 2000 dollars! In America people always act like they have no money! But there is a significant difference in a person who is unwell and on the streets and it is a problem for their health and dignity, respect, self-esteem, ego, pride, and all human traits! Rich people do not seem to care about pride and integrity and any other traits that humans build in this country in the American language! This is heartbreaking and it is sad and depressing for these things to say and to involve. This is affecting all minds and all moods and thoughts!

America is failing, impacting people's lives and poverty existing! In this country there is lots of money that is being spent! You cannot spend money on someone's business, then you have homeless people! Why would rich people exit and poor people? Business is getting wealthy and rich and they believe they are doing stuff for the American people; however, if they are doing stuff for the American people why are there homeless people? Business needs money and money, for you have spent money on communities and spent on building and education, housing, social, all these businesses do believe is for people, but employees do not even understand how much money goes to reversing the thinking: their money spent on their working, housing and education, social services progress, and many other organizations for many years! While homeless people have not accessed employment, education, and if they have education they still have no job because of these issues related to social issues. You have people who are problems and do use their actions affecting their jobs. There are lots of crimes related to businesses who do abstracts of socialism, sending of actions and struggles and socialist programs. These socialism issues, some are major problems in America: slippery and a slap in face, business bureaucracy, capitalism-filled faults, and socialism critics, and directed by central planners and business. Why do they fire? Business fire people? That incentive fire employee will affect people to get the money! How can you have America built on business and against people? Because America has laws, and these laws are interpreted by businesses that they can use it against people and using against them false accusations and firing people or not good enough clams! Laws interrupted are for people to have safety and rights, but businesses using this interrupted them having what they want and if people do comply to their rules, then they evil fire them! Rules they make judgment after they are ended from the jobs, it is not working out the same way! There are just lots of businesses firing employees for cases being late or medical leave or being sick or other gender issues, sexual harassments and grooming gap, and these businesses make up their firing employees!!

Men, I have heard about them feeling they are stupid and their boss firing them being stupid! So, this harassment, same gender, and it is when someone takes advantage of another person! There can be lots of issues because challenges facing workplaces and fact, it's business and related to income and then being fired you face a devastating impact. So, there are lots of reasons that devasting impacts can occur! There are lots of devastating impacts of losing jobs and suffering! These businesses are violating human rights and causing homelessness and any other impacts that exist! More money, there are many businesses they service and more money, better services, but being homeless there are really no services and no solutions! Homelessness cancels all solutions and services! In the country where someone lives, human rights must be bound and something like this should be used to commute the responsibilities! If someone lives in their country, they should have rights and those rights should not be violated! The things, the way Americans have opinions they are all violated, and laws do not work, and they are not equal!

Americans do not believe laws are equal! So, there are still rights for humans but they feel they are violated and abused and there is no point in these laws!!

Regardless, these laws do exist and there are employees who are employed who are in charge of preventing these issues and justice!!

Homelessness is a tragedy. We are obsessed with domesticity in this play of ability to live and not suffer ... we are exposed to confusion and experience by the homeless and disturbed.

Homeless people feel they lose hope! They feel like they lose faith!

A teenager in a Chicago documentary said, "I'm fine, I am fine, I am fine, I am fine, I am fine, I am fine, I am fine, I am fine, yes, yes, yes, yes."

New York Barton Gellman: "I mean that January 6 was not an event that was part of a coherent plan and could oversee to overdose on the left for considerable time in central."

News reporter: "What are some examples?"

Barton Gellman: "One example is that they're seeking out visuals with his players partnered with his players."

There are inequalities in America and there is wealth and poverty in America! There are gap income, gender inequalities, healthcare, and social class issues! There are changes, the worst, the decline of values of the wages, and it has boosted but there are different wages, I mean increased minimum wage. People have lost income when they reach retirement age! So, this is about all wishes. You have poverty minimum wages going up and your lost retirement ages and loss of jobs! There are other losses and even before retirement age! People now are older aged because of jobs, payments and duties of bills! So, they are not flexible for being stable and retiring. A lot of people in poverty have options of vacations and living life meets their health alone, never mind leave pay and vacations! So, it is hard not having a job that is paying enough!

Trends of inequality is this and fact: Overall some people get paid leave and others do not! Some even get to leave if they are sick, others do not! People have issues of not only not leaving while they are sick, but they are being shamed and affected by their boss or someone abusing them for their quality of life and traits!

Income inequalities in the United States are Congressional Budget Office (CBO) measures. Taxes and transfer, but income is lower and market income is highest and other inequalities in the population and how this is a distribution of values of a particular variable.

"U.S. tax and transfer policies are advanced and thus lessen beneficial income inequality. The 2016 U.S. Gini coefficient was .59 based on market income, but was reduced to .42 after taxes and transfers, according to Congressional Budget Office (CBO) figures. The top 1% share of market income rose from 9.6% in 1979 to a peak of 20.7% in 2007, before falling to 17.5% by 2016. After taxes and transfers, these figures were 7.4%, 16.6%, and 12.5%, respectively."

— Chapter 4 —

The Failure of Socialism and America

One person Sapien: from right to fail, documentary says. I was scared.

Um, I did not know anything I was overly concerned about at expense of and misery of the people leaving the adult home. I felt like a human being for the first time."

Tomislav: "How long since you got your apartment?"

"Maybe three month, I'm not sure."

Other people spoke of her feelings.

No one really explored what it looks like when people leave, no, when people leave by the 5th.

People with mental issues and who had their freedom housing and Nora, speaking of one of the people like "Mother loved him and the first time him, just loved him. When he was losing mentally, she began showing signs of agony, losing her only child to mental illness!"

This heartbreaking story, and again it triggers psychological trauma and affects my agitation and anger because of personal reasons of begin mistreated and experience with breaking, being falsely treated. I have mental illness and then "faking that my illness is real, it's in my head and my factitious disorder."

It triggers anger, a form of abuse, and falsifies things in my head, and I have mental illness, but that's because of abuse and using my anger against me and my weakness and my vulnerability against me and abusing me and accusing me of things and then lying about it. It's in my head!! And my age vulnerabilities, weakness, and old people take advantage my own life and to do right, they affect solutions and they have been affecting me since age eleven and they continue the same as when I was eleven behaviors! They are old, and they are having problems with development and behavioral problems and again as a child in Georgia we do not see problems in adults! It is really issues in America and American adults and their development and mental issues and drug usage and behavior and unethical and immoral and unethical behavior in adults!!!! The origin of adult personalities, which in Georgia this is not related to bad personalities! (In America adults relate to bad and roles of adverse experiences of abuse when they were infants and influencing adults' personalities negatively.) They interact illness with related health and social issues and parenting and any relationships.

Lots of threats in my life and abuse by people! Yet (factitious disorder imposed on me) if I can go just get drugs, I want to fix my issues! Drugs do not make, and drugs are not fixing housing, and this article points out that there are four diverse types of justice: distributive (determining who gets what), procedural (determining how fairly people are treated), retributive (based on punishment for wrongdoing) and restorative (which tries to restore relationships to "rightness"). All four of these are … drugs are used the wrong way or for medical emergencies or pleasure! Drugs for emergencies are worse enough, never mind fake-ass people trying to mock me and bully me and act like drugs fix me! Drugs do not fix people and only affect people's anatomy. I find criminal acts of people who think they are going to affect my anatomy and mind! But also, humiliations are that they have wasted my time with their abuse and fake justice and fake actions and wrongdoing.

Some people, they have wasted time, and they cannot restore my time and my life and my age, my situations. These people can never restore any situation and event. It is upsetting, there are so many abusive people in America, and they are never going to fix any problem and social dimensions, social and economic, and legal justice. They are never going to fix sick people they have influenced and abused. Some people in America will never fix anyone by their wrongdoing. That is why punishments are justice!

The Failure of Socialism

The common argument against socialism is that it simply does not work. It is an inefficient system that has destroyed societies and resulted in famine and death. This, of course, is true.

Is Taxation Ever Allowed?

Some will respond, "Following this logic, are not all taxes and government programs theft?" One response is yes, which has some appeal due to its consistency (the view of anarcho-capitalism). However, a more biblical response is that some taxes are legitimate because some government functions are legitimate. Thus, we need to understand the proper role of civil government.

Religious Christians do not want to govern to help the poor. I am not saying it's truth, but some people believe that and anti-socialists. Some people think wealth is not good and it affects socialism and the Bible does not support the wealthy to enter the kingdom of God. Haha, I am not sure if it is called that!

Is Capitalism Worse than Socialism?

The verdict is in, and contrary to what socialists say, capitalism, with all its warts, is the preferred economic system to bring the masses out of poverty and to make them productive citizens in our country and in countries around the world. Remember this: Capitalism rewards merit, socialism rewards mediocrity.

"No one can serve two masters; for a slave will either hate the one and love the other or be devoted to the one and despise the other. You cannot serve God and wealth" (NRSV, Matthew 6:24).

Rabbi says of experience and young people: "Government took over agriculture," but of course Imam from a German public broadcast says, "So it's a wave, it's a wave, all the way of histories trees freeze store, which all then which bullet coming, but it's arming but a preponderance that if the majority of which bullet is coming forth historical or oracle, real reality or reality Christian."

"True faith means holding nothing back." Did Jesus exist and was he *part of socialism?*

Some Evidence!

Earlier this atmosphere consisted of those guests. The Stanley Experiment would not work and he found that he couldn't form any amino acids at all, so the investigation fell apart. Once you use a better realistic Miller's test, it has been reiterated many times using the correct atmospheric components and the results are always the same that generated so much confidence in 1953. They did not appear, Miller's experiment was invalid, you're still light years away from making life. It comes down to this: No matter how many molecules you could produce, conditions possible conditions, nowhere near producing a living cell, and man says, "Here's how I know if I bring a sterile test and I put in a little bit of fluid with just the right salts, just the right proportion of acidity and alkalinity, just the right temperature, the excellent solution for a living cell, and I put in one living cell, the cell is alive, it has everything it needs for life. Now I take a sterile needle and I jab that cell and all that stuff leaks out into this test tube, having this good little test too, the molecules are needed for a living cell, not just logical."

Type of cell they are: All cells have a cell membrane, which separates the inside of the cell from its environment cytoplasm, and DNA, which is the genetic. There are two broad categories of cells, the first category is eukaryotic cells.

Yes, Jesus did exist, and Jesus Christ was wrapped after his death. God was the source of the father's portion of Jesus' DNA, which is entirely consistent with the biblical description of his being the father. He is the father.

Biology, Socialism?
This study compares capitalism and socialism.

People's opinions, the reason the changes happen in medicine and healthcare, are related to the centralization communist-inspired care services and socialized medicine, which is the most important part of establishing communism. Also when you control their healthcare, you control their lives, a collective uprising of the people.

"Government became involved in Medicare or healthcare for the aged in the 1990s under President Lyndon Johnson. It only added healthcare to Social Security and pensions offered by the corporations as settlements to communist-inspired union disputes with these benefits, then became established entitlements. The people believed that the government owed him these entitlement programs, upright. These programs now have costs that go way beyond what can be provided as promised by the politician."

Discussion: "American medicine: His life was altered here and what is called the largest medical city in the world, the Texas Medical Center in Houston. Here doctors test unnatural organs built from scratch, technicians design robots to speed efficiency, surgeons use virtual fact (child health and illness) reconstruction to see tumors inside the body before ever making an incision, and kids like five-year-old Cayson Cox come back from near death. Cayson was born with only half his heart functioning. Normally those hints of blue in his skin are a sign of a little body hungry for oxygen. Most kids with this condition don't live very long, so I can remember it perfectly. It was pouring rain outside, of course, and I was by myself and my doctor told me that she saw that case in the heart was underdeveloped, it was underage every few dark days (sick children and depression and sad life) for me but using new and highly complex surgical techniques, Doctor, that's him on the right, change the course of cases, life case, and 'was going to die' (which will cause pain on the family and everyone) and had we done what we've always done, he would have had it transplanted already or it's a hard thing to say but he would have passed away already but now we have a normal child."

In front of us the doctor came out with the biggest smile on his face.

People who suffer from insurance and medical issues, a person said about COVID-19, "Instead if that were to us, we do not have medical insurance." A group of people to talk discrepancies that the pandemic would worsen, many in the black community felt the healthcare system was not on their side. One person said, "You know from the poorest of the poor to the richest of the rich, we don't get the same quality."

The United States U.S. healthcare system is reluctant if we do not it anything, constructed many factors.

Education, doctors, the overspecialization and affidavits, the statement of discoveries into clinical or among them.

Oversight of studies and importance of concepts, health and research and influencing on the economy, society, public health. Researchers' decisions in health and costs, impacts.

Some major questions in most high-income neighborhoods yet political measures to reduce costs have so far remained ineffective and have damaged the best interests to patients and residents. We therefore investigated the chances to evaluate healthcare systems as a socially established complicated adaptive system (CAS) and founded by the very quality such CAS tend not to respond as anticipated to top down interventions as caps have emergent aspects. The focus on the driver's purpose, economy and behavioral norms requires particular understanding, first the importance of understanding the purpose of healthcare is modification of health and its experience has been emphasized by two recent complementary redefinitions of health and disease. The economic models underpinning today's healthcare profit maximization have shifted the focus away from its main purpose.

Healthcare financing in the present study was to assume the convincingness of healthcare. This objective was achieved through output such as life expectancy at birth, perceived health status, charindex death from acute myocardial infarction and diabetes.

Health mortality increased; health outcomes are affected. Diabetes is bad and has a significant economic impact related to drugs, nurse care and medical devices and services.

System expands, underscore age, life healthcare, financing systems score expect self. Lets health go, your HCC underscore index amid dire total end 210 quadrillion 209 trillion 208 billion 198 million 169,169 M 8.7213280 32067.39970 382341.904 22.944 Sigma 2 3253692.627914 16199.5552322 454524.6967 hsn 848483786565 M 8.836108 80 470 72770.577339 16515.714 Sigma 1.3728072 696014.84758 789589.9542.

How Is Democracy in America?

The United States is a representative democracy. This compromises that our government is elected by citizens. Here, citizens vote for their government officials. These officials represent the citizens' ideas and concerns in government. When did America start democracy?

The American Revolution then popularized this principle, followed by the Constitutional Convention of 1787, which developed institutions to manage popular will.

President Biden: "So let's remember the reasoning of this decision has an impact much more and to the right to privacy more generally."

Biden has supported abortion rights and opposed federal funding for the procedure, including in some instance cases of rape….

Studies, Beliefs, and a Variety of Opinions

Roughly one million abortions are performed each year in the United States alone. The total abortion-related difficulty rate is estimated to be about 2%. Most complications are deemed minor such as pain, bleeding, infection, and post-anesthesia obstacles. Others are major, including uterine and following hemorrhage, uterine perforation, injuries to adjacent organs (bladder or bowels), cervical laceration, failed abortion, septic abortion, and disseminated intravascular coagulation. This activity reviews abortion complications and their treatments and emphasizes the interplay between interprofessional team members to undervalue the incident of abortion complications and options <u>management</u> and treatment.

Objectives:

Interpret the history and physical exam findings of abortion complications.

Review the experiment of patients that have abortion complications.

Outline the treatment of patients with abortion complications.

Outline the importance of <u>communication</u> and coordination amongst the interprofessional team to strengthen the care of patients with <u>abortion complications.</u>

Religious Perspectives

Since the Supreme Court ruled in Roe v. Wade, the stakes around the future of abortion access in the United States have never been higher. Thankfully, courageous religious leaders such as Rabbi Danya Ruttenberg are advocating for reproductive rights as an expression of their faith and not letting the religious right control the religious perspective on the issue. We know that even if the federal constitutional protections for abortion are nearly eliminated in Dobbs v. Jackson, the faith-based reproductive rights movement will continue, because we know from history that religious leaders helped people access abortion even before Roe v. Wade became the law of the land.

There is no one religious view on abortion. BBC says about religion and abortion: "All the religions have taken strong roles on abortion; they believe that the issue constitutes sincere problems of life and death, right and wrong, human connections and the nature of society, that make it a major religious concern."

People involved in an abortion are usually affected very deeply, not just emotionally, but often spiritually as well. They often turn to their faith for advice and comfort, for justification of their feelings, and to seek atonement and a way to deal with their feelings of guilt.

Because abortion affects heart as well as mind, and because it involves life and death, many people find that purely intellectual argument about it is un-satisfying.

Religion and Abortion

All the religions have taken dominant positions on abortion; they believe that the issue affects deep issues of life and death, right and wrong, human relationships and the nature of society, that make it a leading religious skepticism.

For people involved in an abortion, it is not just a matter that interests a human being and their conscience, but something that troubles a human being and their God.

Legal laws indicate people to feel what is right. Some people feel abortion is right and others feel it is wrong. There are lots of opinions because there are lots of people. Laws are speaking and rules are for the society to enforce. Laws protect our general safety and guarantee our rights as citizens against abuses by other people, by organizations, and by the government itself. We have laws to help provide for our general safety. These exist at the local, state and national levels, and include things like laws about food safety.

There, "religious beliefs give strength to the anti-abortion movement—but not all religions agree."

In front of the Supreme Court building in December 2021 in Washington, asking institutional rights to an abortion granted in Roe v. Wade, employing unusually harsh language, Alito proclaimed that bro and Planned Parenthood versus Casey must be revoked because of the decisions of abusive judicial authority. Roe was egregiously wrong from the start. Alito wrote and its reasoning was extremely weak. He also asserted that neither abortion nor privacy is mentioned in the text of the constitution nor should they be deemed to be deeply rooted in the nation's history or traditions so as to be worthy of protection. As a professor of constitutional law who has taught about reproductive rights for more than 20 years, I argue that <u>Alito's</u> legal reasoning leaves out several established constitutional principles also not mentioned in the text, such as barriers of powers and executive privilege as well as rights that <u>conservatives</u> hold near and dear like the right to marry and parental rights. Read news coverage based on evidence, not Tweets, get the newsletter. Alito's claim that a right to an abortion was entirely unknown in American law until Roe is groundless. Historically abortion was not completely illegal even in puritan New England. The first abortion restrictions were enacted in the U.S.A. in the 1820s and even then they generally outlawed abortions only after hastening the early equivalents of fetal viability, the ability to survive outside the mother's womb. Alito's legal rationales aside, the legal war over abortion is as much a religious dispute as it is a constitutional religious opposition.

Anti-Albertan activists kneel and pray in front of the Supreme Court building during the annual March for Life in 2017.

Andrew Harnik: Most anti-abortion rallies have signs and banners with religious admonitions such as "Pray for life" and "Pray to end abortion today." The Catholic Church has a strong opposition to abortion and <u>contraception</u> is well known; however, in an interesting recent book abortion, in early modern Italy, historian John Crystal Poulos argues that prior to 1588 the Catholic Church's role on abortion was <u>ambiguous.</u>

I cannot pick if abortion should be legal or not because laws must be fulfilled but religion is important too. Everyone has their view on religion and everyone has their own rights, so it is hard picking which one is right and if abortion is right or wrong. I cannot pick between the religious and laws. Morals, something significant and empathy: I feel like Americans since I came in America do not have morals and empathy and there is lots of exposure in moral and nonmoral shame. However, there are still laws and laws might be different from morals and there is religion, and some people think it is not right and not related to laws and it does not obey and religion is not above laws... regardless of that, in America there is exposure of morals broken, incompetence, and violated values and other beliefs. I guess for now people got to pick abortions and have the rights to do abortions to some degree ... there are abortion laws, etc. That is what the rights of humans are today.

Abortion Procedure

One woman and a couple have said that from YouTube, "the LaBrant fam":

"Keep my baby but I also knew that of in school and college and I didn't. I was too scared to tell my family. I was too scared to tell my friends. It was just a lot for me to take in being so young. I remember those moments just being so terrified in school. I remember those moments just being so terrified of just like what the future would look like, what my life was going to look like, just so many things going through my head at that moment and just knowing how hard it was going to be, but ultimately in the end how worth it was going to be. Looking back now, I know for me personally my choice was always to keep my baby but I also know that for others there are choices. It's always hard with others, there are choices said. My choice was to keep the baby.

"So what, if you are watching this and you are thinking should I keep my baby, even though it is too hard, in fact I was in that position. I was 19 when I got pregnant with Everly and I remember just being so scared and I did not know what I was going to do. I was in school and college. I was too scared to tell my family. I was too scared to tell my friends, it was just a lot for me to take being."

In the same LaBrant fam YouTube video. I received these perceptions:

"There is so much passion on either side of the topic. Seems to be no middle ground. Virtually no human conversations. So which and in the midst of it all we truly believe that love is the answer. Instead of your life or pro-choice is it possible for us to be pro-love, is it possible for us to love both the mother and child?"

The Bible will support, love and honor, but conflicts between parents and family do not. There are parents against each other, and children need attention, they do not get as much, and lack of gratitude and feeling ignored and even fighting and abuse!!

There is separation damaging children and families and economy and adverse effects....

Parents' relationship to the children is related to the parents' quality!

Parents fight and it affects the child. I know from experience with my son, my heart is broken for my son getting affected for decades with his father's issues, abuse, stress, and shame! It hurts my heart, my son goes through these issues, he does not have a grandpa, father, uncle because they do not count, and family is not here in America. So, he has nobody that is giving him honor and love and respect! My son has no other family but me to bless him. It is affecting me crazy, my son's experience of emotional abuse and neglect! My son has been embraced and humiliated by his father for years. I have been mentally going insane! I have been abusing things inside my home, punching walls and what not out of anger and screaming out of anger!!! I have almost broken my hands and wrists punching things and screaming and crying day and night!! I have so much anger, I am lucky because sometimes it is depression and I want to kill myself and other times it is anger and I want to kill. That is how bad my anger is! But I am alive! Anger keeps me alive, depression affects me, and I become suicidal! That is what I must go through because of conflicts and impacts of conflicts and damage by losers!

People do act like how I am happy if I am mad! (While conflicts have been showing since coming to America at age eleven so I am a happy person and I always have been.) I am a positive person. Just damaged by losers, abusers, and perpetrators. I have a happy persona and perpetrators cause stuff, not me, and all criminals. I am happy and I carry good, positive qualities, and I am trustful and a good life gives me even more happiness and stuff makes me happy! I can be a good person and be great but I have tough times because I have always been a positive person about delinquents and abusers and all other losers affect me and they create conflicts and damage! I am not a negative person. I am happy and positive and not only happy people make me happy, I was positive when I came to America in 2000.

This picture is not when I was 11 but I was 13 or 14.

This is me on the left and a teenager and my friend's sister Colleen and brother Brian, and they are so precious and the greatest people. They are awesome, these people. They are also great and positive and have always been lovers of God and gracious.

Chapter 5

Socialism and Overly Broad

Represent Democratic is a political doctrine that favors political democracy and some form of a socially owned economy, with a particular emphasis on economic democracy, workplace democracy, and workers' self-management within a market socialist economy, or an alternative form of decentralized planned socialist economy. Democratic socialists insist that capitalism is intrinsically incompatible with the values of freedom, equality, and solidarity and that these norms can only be achieved through the fulfillment of a socialist society. Although most democratic socialists seek an accumulative transition to socialism, democratic socialism can support either revolutionary or reformist politics as means to establish socialism. Democratic socialism was popularized by socialists who were opposed to the back-sliding toward a one-party state in the Soviet Union and other nations during the 20th century.

The history of self-governing socialism can be traced back to 19th-century socialist thinkers across Europe and the Chartist movement in Britain, which differed in their goals but shared a common demand of democratic decision making and public holding of the means of production and valued these as fundamental characteristics of the society they advocated for. In the late 19th to the early 20th century, democratic socialism was also heavily impacted by the gradualist form of socialism promoted by the British Fabian Society and Eduard Bernstein's evolutionary socialism in Germany. Democratic socialism is what most socialists understand by the concept of socialism; it may be an overly broad (socialists who reject a one-party or more insufficient concept (post-war social democracy)). As a broad action, it includes forms of libertarian socialism market socialism, reformist socialism, and insurgent socialism, as well as ethical socialism, liberal socialism, municipal democracy, and some forms of state socialism and unrealistic socialism, all of which share an obligation to democracy.

Political belief or political theory is the philosophical study of government, dealing with questions about the nature, scope, and legitimacy of public agencies and organizations and the relationships between them. Its topics include politics, liberty, justice, property, rights, law, and the enforcement of laws by authority: what they are, if they are wanted, what makes a government legitimate, what rights and freedoms it should protect, what form it should take, what the law is, and what duties citizens owe to a legitimate government, if any, and when it may be legitimately toppled, if ever.

Political theory also confronts questions of a broader measurement, attacking the political disposition of happenings and classifications such as identity, culture, sexuality, race, wealth, human-nonhuman connections, principles, religion, and more.

Rights are legal, social, or ethical regulations of independence or entitlement; that is, rights are the fundamental normative rules about what is allowed of people or owed to people according to some legal system, civil meeting, or moral theory. Rights are of essential importance in such disciplines as law and ethics, especially hypotheses of justice and deontology.

Rights are fundamental to any society and the history of social confrontations is often bound up with ties both to interpret and to redefine them. According to the Stanford Encyclopedia of Philosophy, "rights structure the form of governments, the quantity of laws, and the shape of integrity."

Rights by beneficiary accrued, animals, children, consumers, creditors, deaf disabled elders, farmers, humans, natives, Intersex Kings, LGBT (transgenders), men, minorities, parents (mothers, fathers), parents, peasants, plants, prisoners, robots, states, students, victims, women, employees, youngsters, other groups of rights, Congress association, protection, civil sovereignty, civil digital educations, fair prosecution, food, free migration, health, housing, lexical movement, possession, reproductive rest and leisure, self-security, self-cratering of people, conversation, sexuality, water and sanitation.

Social conflict is the struggle for an agency or power in a community. Social conflict occurs when two or more people oppose each other in social interaction, and each exerts social power with reciprocity to achieve incompatible goals but prevents the other from attaining their own. It is a social relationship in which action is intentionally oriented to carry out the person's own will despite the opposition of others.

Conflict theory accentuates interests, rather than norms and values, in conflict. The pursuit of interests produces several types of conflict, which is thus seen as a normal aspect of social life, rather than an abnormal occurrence. Competition over resources is often the cause of conflict. The theory has three tenets:

Society is composed of diverse groups, which contend for resources.

Societies may portray a sense of cooperation, but there is an endless power struggle between social groups as they pursue their own interests. Within societies, certain groups control specific resources and means of production.

Social groups will use resources to their own advantage in the pursuit of their goals and often take advantage of those who lack control over resources. As a result, many dominated groups will struggle with other groups to gain control. Most of the time, the groups with the most resources will gain or maintain power since they have the resources to support their power. The idea that those who have control will maintain control is known as the Matthew Effect.

An action is an event that an agent performs for a purpose that is guided by the person's intentions. So, driving a car is an action since the agent intends to do so, but sneezing is a mere behavior since it happens as a dominant of the agent's intention.

Chapter 6

Mind and Mental Events, Thoughts

A mind **disorder**, also referred to as a **mental illness** or **psychiatric disorder**, is a behavioral or cognitive habit that effects crucial distress or impairment of personal functioning. Such features may be chronic, surrendering and remind or occur as solitary episodes. Many disorders have been interpreted, with signs and symptoms that vary widely between certain disorders. Such disorders may be assessed by a mental health professional, usually a clinical psychologist or psychiatrist.

The causes of mental disorders are often unclear. Theories may incorporate findings from a spectrum of fields. Mental disorders are usually distinguished by a mixture of how a person behaves, feels, perceives, or thinks. This may be related with regions or functions of the brain, often in a social context. A mental disorder is one characteristic of mental health. Cultural and religious beliefs, as well as social norms, should be considered a diagnosis.
Psychiatric disorder, psychological ailment, mental illness, mental disease, mental breakdown, nervous breakdown, mental health

Major depressive disorder (MDD), also known as **clinical depression**, is a mental disorder depicted by at least two weeks of pervasive low mood, low self-esteem, and loss of interest or pleasure in enjoyable activities. Those influenced may also sometimes have delusions or hallucinations. Inaugurated by a group of U.S. clinicians in the mid-1970s, the term was adopted by the American Psychiatric Association for this indication cluster under mood disorders in the 1980 version of the *Diagnostic and Statistical Manual of Mental Disorders* (DSM-III) and has become widely used since.

The diagnosis of major depressive disorder is based on the person's reported knowledges and a mental status inspection. There lives no laboratory test for the illness, but testing may be done to rule out bodily conditions that can cause identical symptoms. The most common time of outset is in a person's 20s, with females affected about twice as often as males. The course of the disorder fluctuates widely, from one event lasting months to a lifelong disorder with intermittent major depressive episodes. Clinical sadness, major depression, unipolar depression, unipolar disorder, periodic depression.

Major depression significantly affects a person's family and private relationships, work or school life, sleeping and eating habits, and general health. A person having a major depressive episode usually exhibits a low mood, which pervades all aspects of life, and an ineptitude to suffer happiness in formerly satisfying activities. Depressed people may be diverted with—or ruminate over—thoughts and feelings of worthlessness, inappropriate guilt or regret, helplessness, or hopelessness. Other indications of depression include poor attention and memory, withdrawal from social circumstances and activities, reduced sex drive, irascibility, and thoughts of death or suicide. Insomnia is common; in the typical diagram, an individual wakes exceedingly early and cannot get back to sleep. Hypersomnia, or oversleeping, can also happen. Some antidepressants may also cause sleeplessness due to their stimulating effect. In violent cases, depressed people may have psychotic symptoms. These signs comprise delusions or, less commonly, hallucinations, usually unpleasant. People who have had previous events with psychotic warnings are more likely to have them with coming episodes.

An unhappy person may report numerous physical symptoms such as fatigue, headaches, or digestive anxieties; physical complaints are the most popular presenting problem in expanding countries, according to the World Health Organization's norms for depression. Appetite often lessens, arising in weight loss, although increased confidence and weight gain occasionally occur. Family and friends may see madness or indifference. Older pessimistic people may have mind symptoms of new onset, such as forgetfulness, and a more apparent slowing of activities.

Socialism is left, economics and great depression is related to changes in socialism and economics. It's impacting people and affecting countries negatively both mentally and economic depression. One is mind and the other is social and economic depression. Income impacts and employments that affect the agony and the minds.

Chapter 7

Social Problems, Economic Issues, and Personal Life

A **social issue** is a crisis that affects many civilizations within a society. It is a group of common problems in present-day society and ones that many communitive to solve. It is often the outcome of components enlarging beyond an individual's control. Social issues are the source of conflicting opinions on the grounds of what is perceived as immaculately correct or incorrect private life or interpersonal social life decisions.

Personal life is the circuit or state of a soul's vitality, especially when viewed as the sum of personal choices contributing to one's private identity.

Separated from hunt, most pre-modern cultures' time was delayed by the need to meet necessities such as food and shelter through harvesting; freedom time was insufficient. People observed with them social roles in their neighborhood and engaged in activities based on necessity rather than on personal choice. Privacy in such communities was unusual.

The recent understanding of "personal life" is a component of recent Western society. Recent people grow to depict their work activities from their personal life and may seek work-life balance. It is a person's intentions and propensities outside of work that define personal life, including one's choice of specialties, cultural interests, manner of dress, mate, friends, and so on. What is special, what actions one engages in during leisure time defines an individual's personal life. For example, a typical American has a

Priggishness is any doctrine with the central focus of applying moral judgments. The duration is normally used as a pejorative to mean "being overly concerned with making moral judgments or being greedy in the judgments one makes."

Puritanism has strongly influenced North American and British civilizations, troubling private issues such as the family part and sexuality, as well as issues that carry over into public life. Of course, sexual assaults are against the moralism and the sex without authorization and coerces, rape and any other types of domestic violence, child sexual abuse and sexual harassments, and it affects people emotionally and psychologically. So, these are against the moralism! Abuse and bodily or verbal abuse is against moralism and violation and rape and discriminatory processes and many others.

Poor and Rich Inequalities

There will be major upheavals by the political social military logical but in terms of health unevenness it thwarts social cohesion.

A black person, aged 28, says, "Hey, disagree if I come home, I collect food and put it aside. Happy first was not seen as something that was."

A white person named Lucas says, "Necessary for growth to Thomas, with something that was crucial for industry for productivity without of it either."

A black man's mind is on his way to work, people look at you.

Black man's mind: *Think they're going to think oh, look at that person, they are picking up that garbage, things like that. You can't let that stop if you have rent to pay and you worry about that your rent doesn't get paid.*

Women's thoughts: *Lucky turn and inequality is actually really damaging.*

The black man lost his job and became homeless (New York, United States): "Lots of people do not want to go to a shelter, I thought this guy has a key to just go in the house and lay on the couch. Homeless people might get robbed, raped, and killed." It is incredibly sad to see Simmons homeless and not having food and beverage and a home and his life being affected by dirty circumstances, including health conditions. This is very impossible to deal with. I wish this man had a better life.

Garbage dumps can provide while others live in slums.

"Why can't rich people help lift those who are below?" (Kenya)

Kenya, North state pensions: 40% of the community lives on less than two U.S. dollars a day. At the same time there are more than 9000 million (about

$28 per person in the U.S.) airs in Kenya. They encompass some of the country's leading politicians. Every afternoon Ochieng sifts through his daily fittings, separating food from plastic and metal.

"Is it in the mail from war?"

"You see these containers? I arrange them on the floor."

"Is it in the mail from war or?"

"You see these bottles?" he says. "I organize them on paper on the floor. I employ a guy who comes in on Sundays and weekdays to wash, clean and dry them. When they look clean and shiny species buy them, we do not regulate. Come on, if I sell these containers today then I might get about 300 to 400 shillings, that's enough to feed my family for today and even tomorrow afternoon before I get back home after work."

Is income of three or $4 a day list going over the international poverty line set by the World Bank at $1.90?

United States is one of the richest countries. It is also home to some of the most glaring quality. As the rich rapidly get wealthier the poorer went ahead to get poorer over, you know, a period of 38 years now. There was massive growth in this country but the bottom 50% Americans, they did not advantage from that growth on behalf of "Sure, we can." A nonprofit recycling center in New York, well, sure we can, that is a unique place when the black man says, "I first came here, I was struck. Here was a place that opened the gates. I see a neighborhood of people, they are all working, cutting boxes, and I looked around and I saw people bring out fresh homecooked food, the trace of it, and I said to myself what is this? They showed me what to do, I thought you just put 24 bottles in a box, no, they said, you want more money sort them. He began to understand to me who was that sister.

"A woman was running this place and right there I said well, there's a touch of God, so now you're redeemed of the five cents and you also recovered the dignity and the value of each human being. Each of us can do a lot given the chance. I don't think anybody here at your weekend wants to live like Wall Street people. We are rich in some way and I think when the persons have the ability to contribute in decision making in surviving their own life that is already ended."

Woman talks: "Forest nations and the richest and in fact when you look at wealth accumulation of prosperity it is rising to a fraction of a global 1% at a tremendous rate."

New York is not just one of the cities with almost 50-year-old movie projectors. Come on, Super 8, Super 88.

"I got to say we, yeah, that's it, that's it, baby, that's it, wow, this is why New Yorkers throw out every single man."

One man from New York: "If you give me three months, I can give a two-bedroom apartment and I am talking about living room, bedroom, bathroom, everything is all out there. When I was a kid my mother had told us, if you can use it again and you save it. And people who do not have enough reserves to feed their kids across a week, right, the gap is getting even more wealthy. People not only elicit more waste than poor people, they also use more of the planet's resources 'cause more, even more wealthy people not only produce more waste than poor people, they also use more of the earth's stocks and cause more already. They also use more of the planet's resources and cause more environmental damage, the ecological footprint of industrialized countries is much bigger than that in the formulating world. I think there are two sides to human prosperity that are so simple."

Woman talks on socialism and democracy: "I have them in my pockets from the one side a bean, everybody needs food, his water, housing, education, healthcare, the basics of distance of life that each person has a claim to and we know these as human rights but at the same time this little blue marble, our planetary home, we need a stable climate, fertile soils, healthy oceans, our protective ozone land so we need to end deprivation and peaks of inequality while creating an endurable future; they go together beautifully."

In Kenya a black person 28 years old: "These TVs and watches are luxury but when you have the money I feel relaxed being here, but since I walked in I have this feeling like I am in a place of a different class. I feel a place where I'm not supposed to be but I also deserve to be here in our news. I've understood lately, I've noticed more shopping malls being built in schools and children's homes. The way I see it they are subsidizing more in malls than in homes and hospitals."

Lakewood, NJ, U.S.A.

Yeah, so the camp goes down this way quite a ways. It's a very big camp, it covers a lot of area and so there's maybe about seven people that live down this way and then there's a nation that lives down this way and except yeah. This is one of our outhouses again, it's a very simple outhouse, it's the old formed just a pit in the ground and with a little building overtop with a toilet seat and so when it gets filled up we just move it over, replenish that one in and start a new one. Level 75 people, these are our neighbors, these are all lovely.

I have never seen anything like that in my life when someone has a car you know and a life, the reality is you know visually they are able to people see roads, you know, the people were able to is their knowledge and that anything while there was crisis or suicide, you know people can witness a crisis and they can witness suicide or industries and they use travel and they use transportation for travel, and that's to be your travel and with your like oh, God, with your traveling with your body and your head so you're able to optimize and basically use the development and America for like services or stuff to encircling your year memory, you're able to use your vision for like services. I have never imagined many places in America. I do not get around and achieve things in America, no money. Money kills traveling. I just never get around.

Paris, if you notice at part of every city in the world every city has some origins. Paris had who lived outside, it was normally the people who lived right around the city entrance or the wall that insured the city during the medieval times. And/or the lands that were either disputed or hard to build on here in New York. Central Park was initially domain in the Upper East and Upper West sides were entirely invaded. In London there were origins. In San Francisco I heard this is not a different historical happening, the squatter buildings were assembled of wood, they were built of equipment that lessened over time and so they disappeared. That means that we do not tend to see this history. The word "slum" is particularly reasonable in the 19th century in Britain but it has been indiscriminately sent out over the entire world and it is completely inappropriate, so I say people have tried to find better ways of communicating.

A woman resident of Bangalore tells about outcomes in India, a man talks sample consistent customers at soon Bello Boston. Well, I'm also frightened one day, this is a slum in Bangalore which is called Lakshman Ramnagar and we have been working here for the past four years. We deal with many cases pertaining to women, children, and husband-and-wife household problems, yeah, that school operates in the middle, dude, just close to the drainage. They have to build their house and they are having a lot of difficulties with their children. They're suffering with lots of diseases....

When it's partly to do with the industrialization of agriculture so that as, of course, if once you start using industrial information, whether it's fertilizer or seeds or whatever it may be, that have to be brought in and it goes on, it evolves much, it's right back, it's rationalized. Nonetheless, the outcomes probably suggest that farms compel less human labor, fewer inputs, so more and more people are omitted from sufficiency from a comfortable live load in the countryside. Naturally they're drawn to the cities where, of course, there is the employment of labor in both the service locality and industrial sector, more doctors we lost, labor one will make the free more....

Socialism solutions? Socialism improves society?

People and Their Stories about Choice, Survival, and Economics
Sexual and religious: To rapid loyalists, fervor are starting up not to work. Who I am and whether I'm good or bad or attaining or not, all its learned along the way, just rod. We can change it any time we want, it's only a choice, no effort, no work, no job, no conservations or money to appreciate if I had the game wrong. The game was to find out what I already was there for. He says you can improve who you are at any time, the way you can change it or that you have opportunity, for example, and nonetheless, I say maybe not. That's where the thing is, no date person is going around, believe that she something, then other day that they did it, the standard time based on the publicly businesses.

Generated a document qualified, unique money mechanics, this newspaper named the institutionalized business money achievement as utilized by the Federal Reserve and the web of global marketable banks it finances on the commencement page. The manuscript states it's factual. The purpose of this pamphlet is to describe the basic process of money achievement in a fractional reserve banking system. It then develops to describe this fractional reserve process through various banking vocabulary, an interpretation of which goes something like this: The United States Government agrees on, it needs some money so it calls up the Federal Reserve, it requests say $10 billion (about $31 per person in the U.S.), the Fed acknowledgments saying sure, we'll buy 10 billion in government bonds from you. So the government carries some pieces of paper, paints, some official-looking designs on them and calls them treasury bonds. Man, it puts a value on these bonds to the sum of $10 billion and sends them over to the Fed, in turn the civilization at the Fed draws up a bunch of outstanding pieces of paper themselves, only this time calling them Federal Reserve notes, also designated a value of $10 billion to the set. The Fed then takes these notes and swaps them for the bonds. Once this conversation is complete, the government then takes the 10 billion in Federal Reserve notes and deposits it into a bank account and upon this deposit the paper notes officially become legal tender money, adding 10 billion to EU's money supply, and there it is, 10 billion in new money has been built. Of course, this illustration certainty transaction would occur electronically. No paper used at all, in fact only 3% of the U.S. supply exists in physical currency, the other 97% truly exists in compute. Now parliament properties these bonds with money at practically developed out of thin air, the regime is entirely promising to pay back that money to the Fed. In other words, the money was created out of debt. This mind-drugging paradox of how wealth or value can be created out of debt or liability will become more clear as we further this training, so the conversation has been made and now $10 billion sits in a commercial bank account. Here's where it gets really interesting for us based on the fractional reserve practice, that $10 billion security instantly becomes part of the bank's reserves just as all deposits do, and considering reserve provisions as stated in modern money mechanics a bank must maintain legally compelled reserves equivalent to a prescribed percentage of its deposits.

Women were under house arrest under Taliban's control, women disappeared from public. Many women's freedom vanished. Female protesters have been shot down. Taliban government ruling. Court ruling, only form of justice system and interpretation of Taliban: "What type of guidelines have you given to people living here?" a woman asks.

"Women should be in the house."

The woman asks, "What happens if women do not obey?"

He said, "She won't be safe."

The Taliban has jailed people ... a young boy who stole something, and he said he will have his hand cut off! This young man is incredibly young and not fed. He was wanting food. He was afraid and soon he might be released. Wardak might be out of the jail. His name is Bizmuller. It might be even not a young boy, so sad. I am not sure about the young boy if he gets out of the prison. It is unfavorable and not a good, that young man might get his hand cut off!

Soviet-Afghan War / Russia in Afghanistan - 1978-1989: Millions of Afghanis killed in collapse. War has killed millions of Afghanis and children. I saw bombs from the air at Afghanis. The Afghanistan war in the Hindu Kush, a war fought by the Soviet Union, prevented Islamic. Like the Vietnan Conflict, dominated by helicopters and airships. Soviets are invaded near the country of Afghanistan. Some United States in Vietnan. A helicopter that affected several of the wars! Afghanistan was demoralized by attacks! Soviets were forced offensive! Rifles they used on births before. Afghanis made firearms and the United States funding paid for the firearms. I am not sure if the United States really did pay for any weapons for Afghanistan, I hate this fact. But I heard it, they did on TV. Helicopters are evasion and interruption. Soviets lacked gun elevation. Lots of people were diminished to live in caves. Food supplies disrupted. They faced natural tragedy. Mujahideen lay ambushed, targeting oil convoys. Afghan troops' lorry has been stopped. Surrender the Mujahideen, order them to throw down their weapons. The Soviet-Afghan War was one of the deadliest conflicts of the late Cold War era. But even beyond abrupt casualties and the inconstancy it brought to the deeper region, the soviet invasion of Afghanistan is one of the most important wars of our times, as it holds an outsized <u>influence on world politics today...</u>

More about the Soviet-Afghan War
The **Soviet-Afghan War** (1979–1989) was a disagreement wherein insurgent groups known collectively as well as smaller Marxist-Leninist-Maoist organizations fought a nine-year guerrilla war against the Democratic Republic of Afghanistan (DRA) and the Soviet Army throughout the 1980s, mostly in the Afghan countryside. The Mujahideen were variously substantiated mostly by the United States, Pakistan, Iran, Saudi Arabia, China, and the United Kingdom; the conflict was a Cold War-era proxy war. Between 562,000 and 2,000,000 Afghans were murdered and millions further escaped the country as refugees, mostly to Pakistan and Iran. Between 6.5%-11.5% of Afghanistan's 1979 population of 13.5 million (about twice the population of Arizona) is estimated to have disappeared in the confrontation. The war inflicted grave injury in Afghanistan, and it has also prevailed cited by professors as a contributing part to the dissolution of the Soviet Union and the end of the Cold War.

The colleges of the tension were laid by the Saur Revolution, a 1978 coup wherein Afghanistan's communists put up with power, commencing a series of radical modernization and land reforms throughout the region. These reforms were unloved among the more established unsophisticated society and established power configuration. The repressive behavior of the "Democratic Republic," which industriously suppressed the opposition and executed thousands of political fugitives, led to the rise of anti-government armed groups; by April 1979, large parts of the country were in open rebellion.

The communist party itself suffered thick interior pursuits between the revolution in September 1979, People's Democratic Party General Secretary man was murdered under orders of the second-in-command, Amin, which soured relations with the Soviet Union. With beliefs rising that Amin was planning to change sides to the United States the Soviet government, under Commander Leonid Brezhnev, agreed to deploy the 40th Army across the border on 24 December 1979. Arriving in the capital, Kabul, they staged a coup (Operation Storm-333), killing General Secretary Amin and inaugurating Soviet loyalist Karmal from the equal group Parcham. The Soviet invasion was based on the Brezhnev Document.

In January 1980, foreign pastors from 34 countries of the Organisation of Islamic Cooperation approved a resolution mandating "the immediate, pressing and unconditional withdrawal of Soviet troops" from Afghanistan. The UN General Assembly passed a resolution protesting the Soviet intervention by a vote of 104 (for) to 18 (against), with 18 abstentions and 12 members of the 152-nation Assembly nonexistent or not participating in the vote; only Soviet allies Angola, East Germany and Vietnam, along with India, benefited the intervention. Afghan insurgents began to receive massive amounts of assistance through aid, finance and service activity in neighboring Pakistan with crucial aid from the United States and United Kingdom. They were also heavily financed by China and the Arab kingdoms in the Persian Gulfs filed by the National Security Archive, "the Central Intelligence Agency (CIA) played a substantial role in affirming U.S. consequence in Afghanistan by sponsoring military operations designed to frustrate the Soviet invasion of that country." CIA covert action worked through Pakistani intelligence aid to reach Afghan rebel groups. Soviet troops occupied the cities and central arteries of transmission, while the Mujahideen waged guerrilla war in small groups running in the almost 80 percent of the country that was outside administration and Soviet control, exclusively being the rugged, undulating terrain of the country. The Soviets used their air power to deal harshly with both rebels and civilians, levelling villages to deny haven to the Mujahideen, demolishing vital irrigate ditches, and laying millions of land mines.

Afghanistan Children Suffer and Are Impacted by War and Fighting and People Suffering

They invaded power and a new parliament was designed at the height of the conflict that attended. There were more than 130,000 NATO troops on the ground, 3500 federation battalions were killed in litigation, 70,000 from the Afghan insurance forces and tens of thousands of civilians. Now after 20 years of conflict, the Taliban again claimed to be in custody of Afghanistan, so how did the war start up, what was Britain's role and why does it last for 20 years? Our idea was clear: The purpose was just our NATO allies and friends rebounded beside us. Taliban needs to make a deal. We'll see if they want to make a deal. It's got to be a real deal, so we went to war against al Qaeda, protect our residents, our friends and our allies. The examination is underway for those who are behind these evil acts. A great people has been moved to defend a tremendous nation. The events of Sept. 11, 2001, shook the world. People watched across the globe as newsreels showed a Boeing 767 slam into the North Tower of the World Trade Center just before 9:00 A.M. in what initially occurred to be a horrible accident. When a second plane damaged the South Tower 18 minutes later, it became clear that this was an attack. A third plane slammed into the Pentagon, just outside Washington, D.C.; and the fourth plane crashed into rural Pennsylvania, after the crew and passengers brought down the terrorists on board. 3000 people were instantly killed in these assaults. The hijackers were terrorists from Saudi Arabia and other Arab nations. The al Qaeda terrorist network, led by Osama bin Laden, was quickly observed as being accountable for the 9/11 attacks. The search was underway for those who were behind these evil acts within ten days (about one and a half weeks). U.S. President George W. Bush declared a War on Terror and stated that overthrowing terrorism was now the world's fight. So what link did al Qaeda have with Afghanistan? He was born in space, 1999, training soldiers were born, the American administration at this time stressing that they hand over all al Qaeda personnel still in the can. Close training in the Taliban military litigation seemed increasingly likely. I don't know the Afghanistan Taliban and issues that they had but I Merrikens unfortunately killed 1000. I'm from saints or millions so the issue was that. Then I heard years ago, I was in my 20s, some American combatants said that we certainly weapon these people. I thought it was a technique, choking it because you can expand their kids, Bob, and so you're saying that you really called them these civilizations. Wasn't there any other way they could help them, like you know who you wanted gad, you thought to have like you know Army procedure....

Actuary Sanctuary and where al Qaeda was headquartered of Pakistan, American sentiment runs high here. Throughout the summer fundamentalist religious parties turned out to protest against U.S. and NATO troops in the region, yes, the ruthless leader of the Pakistani Taliban Baitullah Mehsud had just been killed by an American drone, little I don't feel turn off my face for the first time in the face of these protests, even the Pakistani government feels compelled to condemn the killing of the suit. These taxes have been coming against our wish whether we like or we don't like, they are continuing. You're saying that this was not approved or it was not approved, the position of the government of Pakistan remains there, no drawings, do you support or protest the attack that killed Baitullah Mehsud, the government and the military stance is very clear on this. We consider it that it does more harm than it helps and therefore it is seen by the people as a breach of sovereignty if the U.S. partnership with the Pakistanis is Trump. But Americans' hands are tied but we are not in Pakistan in the way that we're in Afghanistan, we don't have an international in Pakistan in the way that we're in Afghanistan. We don't have an International Security assistance force helping them....

Killing millions suffered, children and lacking necessity, war crimes and prisoners of war, torture and taking hostages... sexual violence and many murders and genocide. This was ethnic cleansing, just about. The aftermath, the was war effects and conflicts: malnutrition, ill and disabilities and post-traumatic stress disorder (PTSD). It is crazy to say I have post-traumatic stress illness when Syria and Ukraine and Afghanistan have the post-traumatic stress disorder. They have been affected by wars! Sexual violence, malnutrition, illness, and disabilities and many other disclosures the war has! What did I go through comparing to Syria, Ukraine, and Afghanistan? I do not know, but it is so disrobing to me, someone accusing of me PTSD and genocide, and I call it genocide, someone who fakes my mental illness and makes up lies about me and is trying to attack me and mistreated me as my race, my quality, values, and aspects and trying to attack my standards and everything! It is crazy exposure devaluing me and lots of Americans do that ... I am angry, susceptibilities of devaluing and genocide.

I am feeling sad about Afghanis and their exposures and the effect of war and their physical issues and children's death and struggles. I am sending my heart to them too. It is so unhappy and weakening.

I wish on the planet that people stop diminishing economic and political hierarchy. Stop affecting people and devaluing people. I wish other countries and every human stops devaluing people and each other and children, keeping children safe and protected and stop affecting the children and abusing them and exposing them to outcomes and killing them, and stop harming their health and stop abusing little children and their environment should be safe and not dreadful and not weakening. Children are presumed to be safe and happy. What men should affect children? Consequence their health? Food and water? No men should impact children and their health and food and water.

I know some men do not think I know the truth and I know anything, but my heart and love speaks, not my brain. I would have memory and suffering of begin broken. Begin broken, you would seek wars because of traumatic memories of armed conflicts. But I am trying to say that I would rather die than pursue war, I would affect men, women, or children. I would protect people if this world did not kill. If this would did not use armed conflicts, I would never kill and I would never kill children. I understand stand armed force defense. I do think men should defend their families and people but not kill humans if they do not have to only defend. Only protection for if someone is trying to kill you. I understand men's impact of wars, pain, and suffering. I understand what defiance is, but wars should be stopped, and they should not happen and that is why we have humanitarian laws. I hope humanitarian laws support a lot, even though they never are enough because wars kill the workers too. War affects them too. Wars are negative and affect people and children, what is important. I really wish men can hear me out even though women are not worried and not contentious like men, but men and women to not be violent and do not be reckless. Be kind and be compassionate and show it to children and think about love, about children and them being safe. Men, think about happiness, not hostility and aggressiveness and other aggressive things and being violent. Think about love and family does not dispute, and even though wars are not one person's fault, administrators need to stop the suffering and the traumatic memories and the effects of the people in this country better and stop the political dispute and importance, only healing and love people not healed through the wars.

Americans and their racial issues are not healed. The poor are suffering, and American life is bad between conflicts between rich and poor. Poor people suffer. I am sure rich people suffer. They pay lots of taxes, and I find that fighting rich people feel like they are being bullied. I am not saying it's truth, but I have heard these things. So, it is not fair, and it is incomprehensible. Americans have lots of conflicts, racial issues and history conflicts, they are never fixed. There are biggest issues harming society … wars are the largest issue in America too. Past wars too and colonial wars and all outside wars. In the United States we suffer from the ethnic confrontations and wars. There are many social conflicts and racism.

We need to stop wars and discrimination in America, and we need to make sure that we never go in the war. Every American needs to be changed as A person and stop conflicts, racism, and wars. only help people in American or outside America. it is okay for Americans to have friends in other countries and it is okay for them to alter and become heroes. Americans need to be heroes. They need conflicts ended and socially become more peaceful. Americans should be powerful and have good forgiving attitudes and be perfectly good. All other countries need to be perfectly good too. Forgiving is a big step because the past was affected by wars and difficulty. Only God knows everything, I am feeling like I am God. But I do hope that all people from all regions and regions and cities are aware of the good and good qualities and being good and remake all their past to help and fulfill the promise and give strength and be faithful. Give us the love, give us the endurance, and help us, not hurt us and damage us. Every country needs to stop the damage and they need to have awareness so love and faith and be welcoming ....

Men need to love and have heart. Men should not hate. People should love not to hate. No people should hate. Do not take worth away from someone. That is hate. Rarest of all men and men hate. Good men love. Good women love.

All worlds should stop being cruel, be kind. Cruel begins with worse and behind. Everyone should only be kind; however, revenge is slander and it's a tragedy. All people, stop the revenge. What good is revenge? Revenge is worse. Everyone should love ... but how do people take good qualities and genes? From parents, and good values and do not let your revenge play in destroying the values and your behaviors….

"The path of vengeance is a messy one with destructive repercussions and often takes many innocent lives in the process."

Do not ever think of revenge and plot it. Work on trying to fix lives. I hope all people are able to stop the revenge and live life with love and desires of love and live positive and happy. Be the people who are helping and saving lives and stop all enemies; do not create enemies and do not go after enemies for revenge. Only protect yourself but never hurt anyone and never time, joy, and life … never take men's life away. It is not legal. It should not be legal to die. Live well.

Match God, his matchless qualities… appreciating! Train men with believing in you and understanding in good and believing in being heroes!

When I got adopted from Georgia. This was the year after, but we went back to Georgia, and this was taken in Tbilisi, the capital of Georgia.

References

https://www.youtube.com/watch V = U Q60RR N UW eight t = 1430 threes HT/W/W / www.youtube.com/watch = HTTPS: // www.youtub.com/watch = SSJJKKMWH TTPS: // www.youtube.com/watch +A2T 5R2

www.youtube.com/watch v = 4 H 1C _6 _Q HTTP W-WW www.youtube.com/re-sults search _ query equals Syria + war HTTPS: // www.youtube.com/watch = sevens at age 9 W Z8 error HTTPS: / / www.youtube.com/watch = U Q60RR NU W8 and T

https://en.wikipedia.org/wiki/War

https://en.wikipedia.org/wiki/Society

https://en.wikipedia.org/wiki/Democracy

https://freedomhouse.org/article/new-report-us-democracy-has-declined-signifi-cantly-past-decade-reforms-urgently-needed

https://www.justice.gov/crt/federal-protections-against-national-origin-discrimi-nation-1